The Doorway

To

Spirit Communication

Channeling

and

Automatic Writing

By

Ashley Marsillas

Contents

Preface

This book is an accumulation of years of spirit communication through many avenues, some with basic meditation and others with channeling and automatic writing. As an intuitive psychic medium, I have had the honor and privilege of connecting with Spirit to deliver messages of love and guidance to many.

I am always amazed that this communication does exist. As a matter of fact, it exists for all of us! Yes, this communication with Spirit is always there for us to use as a way to further our understanding of what is truly possible and to provide answers to the questions of life itself.

I hope this book gives you some understanding of the many ways Spirit communicates with you on a daily basis. All you have to do is be open to the process and allow love and positive energy to flow through you. Once you have an open heart and the readiness to begin, then you can let the Universal Source connect with you and your higher self.

Enjoy.

Introduction

My intention is to describe how to communicate with Spirit, whether it be to connect with your higher self or your family and friends. To begin this process, I will establish the basic principles of meditation and how to set your intention to connect with Spirit. This book will also cover Channeling and Automatic Writing, and I will provide many written examples of these types of communication that I've experienced over the years. This type of writing has been around since Man has been putting his ideas and thoughts down on paper. Or on rock, depending on the time period. (Yes, that was my attempt at humor!)

Enjoy these writings and take them for what they are. They are from a higher consciousness and bring about great awareness if you allow it to unfold as it should. Have fun with this, knowing that there is so much more than what has been taught to us by our parents, teachers and peers. Only our self-imposed limitations can stop us from asking the questions and finding the answers to what is truly possible from within.

Acknowledgements

Thank you to all the wonderful spiritual teachers, mediums, psychics and enlightened people I have met over the years. Your stories and insights have brought a smile to my face and have helped raise my awareness of what is possible if I allow myself to be with the true nature of consciousness on all levels.

I send loving, positive, healing energy to all who read this.

Chapter 1

How to Communicate with Spirit

The very first questions to ask yourself are: "Why do I want to communicate with Spirit? What are my intentions?" If you can answer these questions easily and without fear, then you have begun. Congratulations on this new beginning. There must be a place where you start, but do not be concerned with the result, as this will interfere with what you are doing. In fact, the only ending is your ongoing search for truth and clarity. Just take in all that you can while you learn and grow as the soul that you clearly are. Remember, you are a soul having a human experience, not the other way around. Once you are aware of this, all the rest becomes easier to comprehend.

Now that you are at the beginning and have a clear purpose to communicate with Spirit, you must set your clear intention to do just that. First, you must create this thought and hold onto it, deep within your subconscious. Find a place where you will not be interrupted so you can clearly concentrate on the task at hand. Focus your thoughts on doing this spirit communication with love and positive energy and on talking to your higher self. Do not allow yourself to get distracted by the mundane chatter in your mind.

This is all done with meditation. Through meditation, it is possible to enter into spirit communication, as well as reaching a higher level of consciousness. When you meditate and quiet the mind, your body, mind and spirit become one. This oneness allows you to be in the moment and focus on what you have set your intention to do.

When you meditate, it is of the utmost importance to not be disturbed. Take the time to turn off your cell phone, the computer, or any other devices that might distract you. Your concentration is of the utmost important and taking away any interruptions will help make this much easier and possible. By doing these very things, Spirit knows that you truly are serious about this and you want to communicate with them.

Now that you have quiet and are alone, you are ready to begin. Turn off the lights and close your eyes. When you close your eyes, you start to focus your clear intention to spirit communication. With your eyes closed and sitting in a comfortable position, simply breathe and relax. Let this time be about you and relaxing your body. Allow your troubles and concerns to leave you.

As you begin to relax, start focusing on your breath. Breathe in through your nose and out through your mouth. Really concentrate on your breath and be aware of how your body feels as you do this. Taking about seven deeps breaths in and out should get you into a deep state of relaxation.

Do not be concerned by random thoughts that pop into your head. This is common, especially in the beginning, as you clear away the chatter in your head. Those thoughts are often all the things you need to do once you are finished meditating.

In this fast-paced, busy world, there are always demands on our time and we are pulled in many directions. You may feel like there is not enough time in the day to get everything done. Meditation will help you to slow down and focus on what is essential.

Just allow these thoughts and feelings to be. Simply observe them and do not make any judgments on them. With practice, meditation will help to relax and quiet the mind, so be not disturbed with having perfect results the first time. It will get better each time, and of course the more you meditate, the faster you develop the ability to achieve great results.

Now, as you are breathing and feeling relaxed, the chatter in your head is beginning to subside. You may start to notice things and feel things differently at this time. You may even feel a little alarmed at what you see, feel or hear. In the beginning, all of these experiences are brand new and can seem a little frightening, but there is absolutely no reason to be alarmed.

When you relax the body and quiet the mind, a whole other world often opens up. This is your true inner self, your soul, if you will. The essence of who you really are is right here and has been waiting for you to acknowledge it!

This should get you excited; you are where you should be to find answers to questions that you have. All the wisdom and knowledge are right here from within, allowing you to grow in such a loving and positive way. If you feel excitement and joy, you understand what I have just said. Congratulations on your spiritual awareness.

The next step during this mediation is to set an intention to protect you. This should be based upon your beliefs and what you think will provide protection during mediation. If you are religious, a prayer is appropriate. If you are not, try this example:

"Ask for the white light from the Divine Source and Original Energy to surround you. This white light is filled with love and positive energy. Only positive energies are allowed to be in your space and near you as you meditate. And so it is."

This basic protection has always kept me safe and protected. I have never had a frightening experience when I do this.

Now that you are protected, you must set the intention for what or with whom you want to connect. For example, you may want to connect with your mom, who has passed. Set the clear thought that you want to communicate with your mom and then say her full name. This will put out the vibration of the very thought to her and to the spirit world and realm.

This is important because it will help to activate the Law of Attraction for this very intention. The Law of Attraction is the basic principle that like attracts like, and what you put out, you get back. Thus, you are putting out this intention to communicate with your mom.

When you do this, the energetic vibration of intention goes out to her and she will know that it is coming from you. When you do this intention, please send her love and positive energy. Also, thinking happy memories of her is of the utmost importance. The vibration of love and positive energy is tuned into a frequency that reaches anywhere. The vibration of happy memories is a positive high vibration that reaches her easily and affectively.

Since you are still in the physical realm, you need something to relate to, to communicate with our example. Imagine you are sitting on a nice, comfy chair in the garden, surrounded by beautiful flowers. There are two chairs there and you are in one of them. As you are sitting there, you notice how perfect the weather is and how beautiful it is. The temperature is perfect, the sun is providing a delicious warm glow. The sky is a light blue color and has no clouds. There are butterflies, hummingbirds and little creatures playing about. The scene could not be more idyllic.

As you sit there, you feel a presence and know that it is your mom. She sits down in the other chair and smiles at you. You both speak without talking, but you know you are communicating.

You are communicating telepathically. The scene unfolds as it should, and you get to experience spending time with your mom again.

This example is very powerful and often brings about intense emotions that you haven't felt in a long time. There may be tears. Let these emotions come out and know that you did have a real spirit communication. Another way of knowing this was a clear communication with Spirit is the temperature changed, or you felt tingling on the top of your head, or on your arms or hands.

When Spirit is present, the energy and atmosphere changes, and your body reacts to these changes. This is all normal and you will be just fine. In time you will feel this regularly and know you are connected to Spirit.

The last step is to thank your mom for communicating with you and to send her your love. Let her know you will do this again very soon. When you are ready to come out of the meditative state, begin to take a few deep breaths and wiggle your hands and feet. Slowly open your eyes and just sit there for a minute, taking in what has happened.

Keep a paper and pen handy as you may want to write this down. You may even want to journal what you experienced during mediation. Fun, right? If you do this safely and with the highest and greatest good, you will be just fine. Make sure you do this with love and positive intentions, always.

This is one of the safest ways to communicate with Spirit on your own. If you are fearful in any way, this might not be for you. If you are afraid of the dark, or of being alone, or whatever the case may be, seeking out a professional psychic medium might be a good option. Remember, using love and positive energy are the most important ways to communicate safely and calmly.

This is just one basic example of how to communicate with Spirit. There are other ways, but all go through some sort of meditation to facilitate the connection. Daily meditation can be fun and so relaxing, and the health benefits alone are priceless. That was just a simple type of communication. Two other ways of spirit communication are channeling and automatic writing, which I will explain in the next two chapters. I'll also provide some examples of these that I have done over the years.

The biggest point to meditation is to relax, breathe, set your intention, protect yourself, and allow whatever happens to unfold as it should. I get some of my greatest information from channeling and automatic writing through meditation. As a side note, it is worth mentioning that automatic writing is also known as spirit writing. I have heard both terms used when describing these writings.

I hope you enjoy communicating with Spirit through meditation. I am always available to answer any questions you might have. If you do wish to meditate, please set aside a time every day for the most beneficial results. Your body, mind and soul will thank you for it.

"Love never dies; neither does that connection." - Ashley Marsillas

Chapter 2

What is Channeling?

Channeling can be defined as a set of concepts and principles that allow you to communicate with Spirit through energies and entities that come into your space. To allow Spirit (or spirits) to communicate through you, you must be willing to give up some control of your physical body by deeply meditating to a very calm and relaxed state.

The amount of energy that is needed to accomplish this is quite intense. Spirit needs your energy and physical body to communicate by using your voice and other physical means. This can be as simple as vocally expressing their words of wisdom or by writing and talking at the same time.

I believe Spirit knows what you need at this present time; I also believe that you inherently know what you are capable of with your physical body. It is of the utmost importance that you set, and trust, your clear intention in order to achieve the highest and greatest good for both you and the spirit energies.

This must be done with love and positive energy to ensure the best and safest experience for all involved. When done with love, which is the highest positive vibration, the results will always be wonderful. An intention set with love and positive energy activates this conscious vibration, encouraging the best match for your vibration to come into your space. The Law of Attraction is activated by these very vibrations and allows such experiences and expressions to flow naturally.

This can be explained thus: When you have a thought, it generates a vibration and goes out to the Universe. The thought vibration will attract an exact match to this energy and will come back to you during channeling. The spirit that is channeling with you can be described in many ways, but we will keep it short for now.

This spirit energy may come very close to you or even be in the same aura/energy field as yours. This space, that is unique to you, will receive this energy and begin to communicate through voice and writing. This process is called Automatic Writing or Spirit Writing, which we will discuss in greater detail in the next chapter.

When channeling begins, your body is usually unaware of any change, other than the sensation of something feels different. In my case, I feel more alive, more energetic with happiness from within. After a session, I'm usually quite wound up, but eventually come down to a normal state of being. It may take a few minutes to gather myself and then I meditate to fully come back into my body and natural state. I usually drink lots of water afterwards and then check what I've recorded (if speaking) or written.

Even after all these years, I am still amazed at the results of these interactions. I know that these communications come from a higher consciousness. These expressions have always been about love, positive energy, and helping others to grow spiritually, as well as refining conscious and subconscious communication.

Our energy from within, the essence of who we truly are, is capable of so much more than what we really think is possible. We have the ability to communicate with spirits, energies, and entities that are no longer in the physical if we seek to do so. This is all possible through meditation.

If you are willing to experience the process of what you can do with your amazing spiritual self, doors will open to wondrous things. These doors can be opened wide or just a crack, depending on your level of trust, knowledge and intention.

When you are channeling, you can either be in control or surrender most of your control to this energy. It's a matter of knowing and trusting that what you are communicating with has your greatest good in mind for you, as well as for all who hear and/or read what is expressed.

This process is something that can be learned with time. Communicating this way with Spirit is a wonderful way of expressing your higher self as well as being in direct conversation with spirit energies and entities. What an amazing feeling, knowing you have the ability to do just that!

You are an extraordinary, physical human being who has the potential to do wonderful things, provided the right intentions lead the way. Helping others and helping them to heal is a great intention.

Sharing this information so others have access to it is another good intention. Remember to do these communications with love, positive energy and respect. The results can be quite profound.

Preparation for a channeling session is very important. For example, I gather everything that I need for the session beforehand, such as a notebook, pens, recorder, water, etc. I encourage you to keep everything within easy access so there will be no hunting for things during your session. It will break your concentration if have to you stop to go get something you need.

Once you have everything in place, you then set the clear intention for this channeling session. Go somewhere quiet so you will not be disturbed and make sure all cell phones, computers, etc. are off. You want nothing to distract you during this time. Get in a comfortable chair and meditate. Use the example in Chapter One, if need be.

Basic meditation to begin is very important here. Make sure you surround yourself with the White Light from Source and ground yourself down. Open up your chakra areas and connect to the Universe and the Earth.

Set the loving intention for your spirit guides to accompany you during this experience to keep you safe and aware. Now invite these spirit energies into your space to express themselves and communicate loving and positive messages for the highest and greatest good.

Once this open channel of communication has been established, you should have the sensation that you are ready to begin. A natural understanding will come over you as to whether this session should be recorded or written, and you will automatically do what Spirit wants you to do. Express yourself in whatever way seems to fit this session and just go with it.

Just allow yourself to speak or write whatever comes to mind. Let this experience flow naturally and allow yourself to be with what it is. Let it unfold as it should for best results. You will know if you should keep going; likewise, when the flow of expression feels complete to you, you will know you are done.

Once you are done, make sure to thank your guides for their communication with you. Send them your love, respect and gratitude for this experience. Go back into a mild meditation to end the session. When finished, I suggest you get up to stretch and walk around a bit. Come back fully into your body and return to your normal state of feeling. Drink some water and then go see what was written or recorded.

Do not judge what is written or spoken. Simply acknowledge what this experience was and allow yourself to think about the message that was sent. Allow your feelings and emotions to be what they will after you hear or read the material. This message was meant for you and you should feel honored that there was communication of some sort.

In my case, my automatic writings are no longer than four to eight minutes long. My recordings are usually around three to five minutes in length. Your experience will be different, so do not set a time frame for this. Your physical body will let you know when it is time to end the session. You must trust your body to know the difference between how you feel normally and how you feel during these sessions. This will gauge when you have had enough.

I've found that a session does take a physical toll on my body, but it might not for you. However, it is better to be safe than sorry. So, for your own health and well-being, listen to what your body is telling you. The results of your session will also encourage you to do this more often.

Channeling is often thought of in a negative way, either because of the belief systems we formed as children, or from what we learned from our parents, teachers and peers. If you think, for any reason, that channeling is wrong, evil, or scary, then perhaps you should not try it.

I do everything with love and positive intentions and I have never had a negative or scary experience. I live my life based on love and positive energy. Anytime I do such things, I make sure to have the highest and greatest good intentions for all involved. This always works for me and I suggest you do the same. Just put these intentions into your own words and make them work for you.

This form of spirit communication has been a wonderful way for me to grow as a spiritual being and as a person. I feel like my life has changed drastically, for the good, since I have had my spiritual awakening years ago. Channeling is done many ways, and different environments may teach and show you differently. What I have explained is what I do and what has worked for me specifically. I encourage you to do your own research. Google "What is channeling?" and discover where you resonate with your findings.

Be proactive and take the time to find information on your own. The internet is an endless source for videos and websites. There is a world of information out there at your fingertips. Take advantage of these amazing technological times that we live in. It will benefit you in many ways.

I can always be contacted if you have questions. My website information will be under the *About the Author* section.

Chapter 3

Examples of
My Channeling

Here are a few examples of some of my channeling sessions over the years. They may read a bit differently, as they must now be put into words. Please just read them for what they are - recordings of my channeling. I was told to write them exactly as they are, even if the grammar and sentence structure is incorrect by our standards. I hope you get something profound from them to assist you in your life. I wish you well.

These were channeled through me by my Spirit Guides and Ascended Masters. I believe the collective energies from my Spirit Guides and Ascended Masters have given me these wonderful channeled sessions. This is done with Love, Respect and Gratitude.

There is a vibration that resonates with you at this time. This frequency coincides with the energetic vibration of Love and Positive Energy. Thus causing a very higher source of connection to Source Energy and all realms of wisdom and knowledge. Let your linear experiences flow naturally and allow the unfoldment of the Universal Consciousness to bring about healing energy to all. Receiving this communication is imperative to the conduit to share these linear expressions of information at this present time. Give the exact messages as they are given to you and do not dilute what is said in any way shape or form. Let these higher expressions of communication be the frequency of Love, Positive Energy surround you in the beautiful Golden/White Light. This Golden White Light imparts the Truth and Clarity necessary to help others on a very profound and meaningful way. Be the one to truly help with the clear message of Love, Positive Energy, Happiness, Joy and enlightenment to bring about healing on many levels. Be as it should and let the unfoldment to commence now!

Exist with Love

Another Channeled Session in 2016

Receive this wisdom and knowledge with clear understanding of our expressions at this linear time. Know the consciousness does exist on a higher plane and brings forth truth and clarity. Allow our collective energies at this present time to express our communications now. The emotions of the physical are brought about by a deep rooted trauma and/or issue that is not released in a healthy expression. These blocked areas of energies must be flowing naturally to allow for healing on all levels. Individual Spiritual growth is always a choice that must be done with Love and Positive energetic vibrations from Source! Once the natural flow of allowing is perceived, then one can come to rational and truthful decisions in the linear lifetime. Know the true self is purse energy and is always trying to express itself in its natural form. This can only happen when balance and harmony are as they should be to receive the most wonderful experiences possible. You as a physical being must know you are that true inner spirit waiting for the opportunity to be awakened from within and be who you truly are.

Exist in the Reality that is now!

An Example of Channeling in 2018

The value of this present moment is immeasurable. This experience of clear communication at this linear presents an opportunity to bring healing to all who hears and reads this. Your existence in the physical is allowing such Spiritual growth for all involved. Your traumatic experiences, as you call them, bring awareness on a higher plane of being to allow such expressions of Love and Light to activate the true Spiritual Awakening from within. When this Awakening happens, a energetic shift begins a new linear of self discovery, for not only you, but all involved in your family and friends dynamic. This group of Souls feels this shift of growth on all levels to make for a better experience for the tomorrows of this physical lifetime. Be the one to accept what has happened and learn from those experiences and let thy true inner self lead the way. Healing is only possible if one allows such experiences to shape them in a positive way from all types of expressions, both negative and positive. Give into the learning experience of life as a physical being and know one day soon, the answers one seeks will be available to them. For this present moment is all that is possible for each and every one of you now. Live knowing you must have these experiences to come to your own awareness and hopefully growth, to allow the path towards enlightenment. Live now and be with oneself in the present and express the energetic vibration of Love, Positivity and Joy. This is possible if you truly allow it to be.

Exist

An example of Channeling in 2017

This is a very special time right now. We can communicate with you through your body, your voice, your vocal cords. We can communicate and give you messages of Loving Light and positivity in all ways through you. We channel through you now at this linear and send you Love and messages that are meant for you as well as all who hear this. This is a positive time filled with possibilities of communication from the other realms, from the Spirit World and where we are from! All of our energies have collected together to communicate with you in this linear experience. You are actually receiving these messages now with love and enlightenment from us that have come before you. We allow these energetic vibrations with experiences and knowledge that must be told to you now at this very present time. The first thing that must be told to you is you must accept these frequency collectives of that energetic vibration of Love and Positivity and all that is right now. Do not wait. Do not question and let the unfoldment to allow your Spirit to take over and to accept these messages in the present! Allow the energetic vibrations of Love come in right now. Let them come and take over for it is truly who you are. Your Spirit within is an amazing energy that is ready and able to do exceptional connections on a very high plane of frequency. Exist with Love and let the unfoldment begin!

I wish you well

Chapter 4

What is
Automatic Writing?

Automatic Writing is a means of receiving the basic principles and concepts of spirit communication through your writing. This can be done in a very simple manner or can be as prolonged an experience as writing a novel. Again, before you try this type of writing, be sure to set the clear intention of doing this with love and positivity, and only allow that which is for your highest and greatest good to enter your space. Once this is clearly set, then you can try this type of writing. It is best to begin with a meditation and then formulate a question that you want answered via automatic writing. This is the most basic beginning for written spirit communication.

Asking for guidance from your spirit guides and/or guardian angels is always a good idea. Whatever makes you feel safe and protected is fine, as long as you do not have feelings of fear. This must be done with love and positive energy or you might not get the results that you seek.

Automatic writing can be a fun way to communicate with Spirit if you so choose. This is also known as communicating with your higher self and subconscious. Your inner self, your soul, has more answers than you realize. You are wired to be able to access this area of your mind, if and when you are ready.

It is imperative to acquire the wisdom and knowledge of the basic ideas of this form of communication in order to get positive results. Think of this as a new experience and simply try it to see what happens.

When in doubt, stop and do not do it again. But if you do not have any fear of communicating with the spirit realm and/or your higher self, make it a fun experience and start writing.

Automatic writing can be channeled from Spirit and can be quite intense; it depends on your intention and what you are trying to accomplish. I use it for many things, but mainly to achieve the highest level of communication as an intuitive psychic medium and spiritual teacher. I invite Spirit to come into my space and write what they will and allow the letters to flow onto paper without question. I am always astonished at what is written when I do not let my ego and brain get in the way. When you allow a clear path of communication and do not interfere with what is being presented to you, the results will be wonderful.

The simplest way to begin is to ask a few questions and write them down on a piece of paper. Have these questions by you when you want a written response. Again, I ask you to please meditate before any session and set your clear intention, and you will get good results.

After you meditate, get your paper and pen ready to write. Ask your question or questions by writing them out again. Ask for direct answers, because when you do this, it puts a clear intention on what you are trying to accomplish.

It is important to follow a basic routine and an order of things, especially in the beginning. To signal your clear intention that this session is for the automatic writing, try set aside the same day and time for this purpose. As you become more comfortable doing this, you can make the necessary changes to allow this flow of words to come to you more easily. With time and practice, an easier communication with Spirit and/or your higher self will come.

For the most positive results, I recommend using a journal dedicated solely to your automatic writing. This sets your clear intention that you are serious about this form of communication. It gives that extra energetic vibration so that Spirit and your higher self knows that you have a good purpose for these writings.

The greatest challenge is to just allow what comes to you without question. Our ego and consciousness try to take control and get in the way. You must not allow that to interfere with what is being written; this comes from a higher knowing! When you just write what comes to mind, then you are getting pure messages from Spirit and/or your higher self.

True automatic writing usually seems like someone else is writing or talking to you. Words and phrases that you would normally not say or write are often given during this session. Do not be alarmed; this is normal. Your higher self and spirit communication writes differently from the way you might ordinarily think.

Sometimes you may even have to look up a word to find out the meaning. This is really a good sign - to see writing that doesn't look like your own. Provided the message is a loving and positive one, then by all means continue and enjoy this new form of expression.

This should be fun and a new way of getting answers to your questions. It will be exciting to see what is possible when you see what appears right in front of you on paper. Many authors and writers do this without knowing what is happening. This is called "in the zone" or just writing without effort. Most writers don't even know this comes from their higher self and/or Spirit. When the words are flowing, and the writing comes naturally, that is when they say it is the most fun and enjoyable. This can happen to you, too, if you are considering writing a book, a novel, or simply looking to express your creative side. Enjoy the experience and see what happens with the automatic writing.

Please know this is a prime example of what is truly possible from within, if we allow our soul to take over and expand our horizons. We are capable of so much more than we think. Experiment and be open to the possibilities. A whole new world is waiting for you if you open this doorway to spirit communication. It is not evil or bad: It is a way of expressing yourself with a higher consciousness. Do not be bound by fear. When you base your decisions on love and positivity, many doors open in a good way. Allowing new experiences to be a part of your everyday life will bring you to more learning and knowledge.

I would like to make mention here of the Law of Attraction, because everything is energy, and everything vibrates at a certain rate. The vibration that is you and your space will attract that which is like you. Like attracts like. What you focus on, you will receive. If you are a positive, upbeat person, you will attract that type of energy into your space when automatic writing. But if you are negative and live a fear-based life, that is what you will attract. I ask you to please be mindful of your energetic vibration is and be aware of what you might attract, depending on what you send out.

My goal is not to scare or frighten you, but to bring awareness to what is possible; the goal here is to bring love and positivity through your automatic writing. If you do that, you will be just fine. As a matter of fact, this will help you grow as a person and as a soul. Learning something new is always an exciting adventure.

Take this new experience and have fun with it. All things can be done with fun, if you remember to set your intention in a loving and positive way. Self-expression is one of the greatest gifts that we have in this lifetime. Allow yourself to be open and try new things and you will be surprised at what you are capable of.

Spirit communication should not be something to be feared. It should be looked at as something that we all can do with love and positivity. I repeat this phrase often, as that is the highest form of vibration out there: love and positivity.

These words vibrate at such a high frequency that it puts out an instant connection of protection around us, like being surrounded by a white light filled with Love and Positive Energy.

If you are content with simply reading about automatic writing and not trying it for yourself, that is okay as well. You should only try it if you feel compelled. You will know instinctively if this is something that you want to use, whether to raise your self-awareness or to discover what is possible through spirit communication.

I say this again: This is not for everyone. You should have a strong desire to try automatic writing and want to communicate with Spirit. If this is the case, please follow the basic steps I have outlined for the process and do it with a calm and clear intention for what you seek.

"Find the clarity in truth. When you are clear, the truth will be revealed." - Ashley Marsillas

Chapter 5

Examples of my Automatic Writing

These are a few of the many automatic writing sessions I have had over the years. I believe that these writings are from a higher source, as well as my spirit guides and ascended masters. It is my deep hope that you receive some helpful information in these written words from Spirit. Again, these words are exactly as given to me, so some of the grammar or spelling may seem unfamiliar.

The automatic writing that I am about to present to you is from 2016 – 2018, the present as of writing this book. They are just some of my many writing sessions, which I always begin with meditation and setting the clear intention to write what I am given.

Afterwards, I meditate to come back down from the energetic vibration that is with Spirit. Spirit vibrates must faster than we do in the physical. Read the words and take what resonates with you. I wish you well.

Look deep within yourself to find the answers that you need. All is possible if you open yourself to Spirit. Your Soul is a very loving, powerful entity to help you with all that you seek. Listen and see with your internal ears and eyes, for they transmit the truth! Go within yourself to release fear, doubt, shame, angst, sadness and all lower vibrations that do not match what you are capable of doing to help others as well as yourself. You as a physical human being have limitations, but your true self, your Spirit from within, has unlimited potential for all things that you desire. Seek the answers you need, but live your life in Love, Happiness and Understanding of what is.

Live, Love and experience all that you can, as this linear expression that which you call life, is over in but a blink of an eye from our perspective. You have that which you call time, a concept that we still do not comprehend, but know that it is a three dimensional expression of what you in the physical have created in your paradigm.

To you and all who read this

I can feel such energetic vibration from you. It is in such a manner that it permeates sadness and confusion. Find the balance to Love and Joy with communications to both realms. There is Love and answers to all realms and dimensions. Positive, Loving Energy is what you seek and is all that you need. There is such happiness in the truth found from within you. Go with the true essence of life from within and let others be aware of this existence. Life continues in such a manner, that it is hard to describe in your language. The expressions, you call words, do not describe what and how we perceive our existence to you in the physical. Live with true Loving intentions so much more will be available to you to access in your linear. You are meant to learn all that is needed in all energetic frequencies such as positive and negative. Be and live with knowing there is so much more than this physical lifetime. Until we meet in Spirit, Live, Love and be true to yourself in all aspects of life as you go on this experience you call a life time.

Love to all who sees this

There is much to be said about the experiences that you feel each day. These are affecting everyone in your life including yourself. Take the feelings and energies of these experiences and align your Spirit with growth and knowledge. Learn from them by living and being in this realm that you call Earth. Feel the energetic vibration of these situations daily and act upon them with Love and Compassion. Know to truly exist, you must go through these linear methods of living to truly understand your path. Be yourself and exist Love, Kindness, Compassion and all will be revealed to oneself in time. Be you and experience all you can, for this lifetime is but a fleeting moment. Know there is so much more, but for now, live in this realm of Earth and exist with Love.

And so it is

You are experiencing this life as a choice that you made. It is made up of expressions and experiences to help you grow as Spiritual entity. To feel the vibration of this plane is both painful and limiting while in the physical, but can be joyous as well. There is a time when you choose to move on and that time and that time arrives sooner than later. It is upon these experiences that you will learn to grow from within and to help others grow. It is meant for you and others to experience all that is and must be. You are a Spiritual Being that must heal others and start healing yourself now!! Time is of the essence and you must make use of these experiences to grow both Spiritually and humanly. Love thyself and others with great passion and life will become more intriguing each day. Live with such passion and Love that it is absolutely amazing all that you experience.

Unknown signature

There is strong vibrations moving at a very fast pace in your physical body right now. You are at a point in your Spiritual evolution to learn more, feel more, do more with the abilities that you have. Reawaken your true Spirit and become who you truly are. Be the Spiritual and Healing being that you are and can be. Give way to Love, Truth, Compassion, Forgiveness and to express these principles and concepts to all who will listen. Your Spirit and Soul are now in alignment with your true calling and path. Time will seem slow and then fast in your linear experiences. Be steadfast with your decisions that await your actions. Do now, be now, act now and all things coming to be, will be understood by your human emotions. All is and starting to be from the Spiritual Realm from which you come.

Be, Live, Love and Do.

Being complete is a process of living and experiencing life. You use all of your senses, emotions and feelings in the physical to grow as a Spiritual being. How you react can be helpful in any manner. Life is meant to be in all positive and negative experiences. You cannot grow if you do not feel all there is to experience. This is an exciting time of feeling all there is to do, say, hear, know and be. Live your life the best that you can and take in every emotion, feeling, experience to gather this linear expression of living. Raw emotion and experiences can produce such grand results that you must endure the rough, bad times to appreciate when all is well. Be and Love this time of living, for it is over so quickly in your linear world. Live it to your fullest of your very being.

Unknown signature

This linear finds you with many questions and concerns pertaining to this lifetime of experiences. Answers you request, but they will be revealed by experiences in your life. Wisdom and knowledge come by experiences, not be being told what this or these experiences are and mean. These experiences are learned by living them, not by asking and being told. Look for vibrations of Love and life, in all that you do and answers will come with your expressions of time. You call this linear, or time and it cripples your existence by living by its limitations. Be, exist, experience and all will come this lifetime with amazing insights and understanding. Knowing only comes from within yourself and life experiences. Be Love, be Happy, be You. For there will never be another you again. Let all unfold for you to discover in time and life experiences from within and from your physical human body. It is beautiful to see, feel and hear all there is to be in this lifetime. Live it for your time goes by so very quickly.

Exist

Your Spirit is awakening at a very fast frequency. Spirituality is who and what you are. Love and feeling all emotions of this existence and what is necessary to become transcendent to another level of consciousness. You will be with others before you, during sleep, meditation, readings, daily experiences and learning all there is to this life. Your particular existence is meant for greatness if you allow it to be. Healing oneself first and then others is the true nature of self. Love yourself and send Love to others to feel the Divine Spark of your existence. Do Spiritual work for all you come across and heal them with Love and wisdom, if they allow it. Then you will feel your true essence in all that you do. Be Love, be kind, be a healing Spiritual being to feel all the Source Energy that is. There is true happiness and inner peace in all that this work is.

Unknown signature

This Earth plane needs humans like you to bring them back to when they truly were connected to Source. The Spirit within is being awakened, for many Souls need the guidance through Mediums, Psychics, Channalers, Healers to help them to know they are having a human experience and that their Soul is eternal. Living a Spiritual life is who we all are. For most of creation, need the clear reminder of who and what they really are. Be steadfast on your journey to realization of your abilities and help others instantly and now! The Earth is in dyer need of guidance from Spiritual beings in these linear moments. Be not confused or sidetracked by such ego, monetary gain, for all you need and desire will be provided to you and for all. Be the strong healing Spirit now and heal all you come into paths with if they allow. There is a great energetic shift and it begins now and with you.

Unknown signature

This day finds you with many questions and seeking clarity and truth. Worries and concerns are for a human experience to develop and learn from. Seeking wisdom and knowledge is for the Spirit to find oneself true inner being. Your true essence whom you truly are within yourself. Seek answers to questions, only if you are ready to acknowledge what you will find is truth and what really is. Be the Spirit that is full of Love and kindness, for this Spirit will find many answers, not only from within, upon many life experiences to unfold. You are on a journey of exploration that must be experienced by the human form and all human experiences that are. Be and live this life with full attention knowing one day, all answers will be available to you. Love, Happiness and Kindness is and what you truly are.

Exist

Your shift in this existence is happening at a vibrational match now. Much is coming to light in these troubled times on your Earth plane. The realm of humans is starting to open up to allow other higher realms of Spiritual Entities to come through more easily. The Love that is possible is and will happen in these times of difficulties. Healers will be stronger and have more of an impact on mankind. Take the wisdom and knowledge to help others believe what is possible of their true inner self. Being in a human body can be limiting, but the possibility of such inner growth is there. Ask to learn and be within to bring forth what and who you really are. Go with Love and Kindness and bring forth Happiness for you as well as all who you come in communication with. For that is who you are!

Unknown signature

The energetic vibrations are strong at this time. Your linear experiences feel the shift in all that is on your Earth plane. Be in the present moment to feel all what is and what will come to be. Your existence and experiences will be a Loving and Happy memory of things from all life times. Live in the present with Love, Kindness, Compassion and this life experience will be beyond what you could even imagine in a fantastic way! To be alive, in the physical, in this time on Earth in a human body, is full of amazing experiences for you and all around you. Be in the moment to feel the true inner being that is you. Love it, feel it, be it. For you know what it is like to be Love, Light and all encompassing Happiness.

Unknown signature

Energetic vibrations of Love and Light are all around you now and always. Allowing them to come through is the hardest obstacle to overcome for a physical perspective. Being open to such receptive energies, allows oneself to truly grow in more ways than we can explain. Receptiveness to these energies allows growth and knowledge on a more Spiritual level in all concepts and aspects. More understanding of life and life's purpose, will allow you to become more aware for individual growth and experiences towards transforming your limitations to enlightenment. Be the Spirit within yourself and give way to growth of self and all around you. Seek not all answers, but seek understanding of truth. For that is true Spirituality in its truest form! Go with Love and Light and much will be released unto you in this lifetime.

Unknown signature

You are experiencing this writing and message at this time, for it is now that it must come through for you at this very present moment. Love and vibrations of peace are at hand. Be not worried about such life situations beyond your control and influences. Focus on the present to be with inner peace and the truest form of inner self realization. The linear time is now to accept who and what you are. Be your Spirit within to help and heal others, if they allow it, with such pain and discomfort in these humanly experiences. Share with them Loving messages from ones that are here and impart comforting wisdom from higher self and realms. You know how to do this and will do so now. Be strong in this mission of Love and Healing to spread the truth of who and what we truly are. We are Spirit Energy that vibrates so Lovingly and strong with Love and great resolve!

Heal others now!!!

These are fascinating times and experiences for you and all around you. Seeing the truth from within is where you will find the answers to this earth plane and experiences of confusion. Clarity and pure Love of self begins the healing and brings you to a higher vibration of understanding and energetic Spirituality that is a match! Be full of Love and Light for that is what you truly are. When such behaviors exist, answers and clarification for many things become available to you. Seek not these worldly answers, but seek the experiences to grow both physically and Spiritually. From within comes clear senses and clear understanding. The experiences of this lifetime brings such growth of fulfillment for your purpose. Be in the present to truly experience this existence and all that must be fulfilled. What you seek is upon you, guiding you and clearly calling you!! Be the Spiritual being of Love, Light and Positivity and share it with all!

Exist

Writing and communicating at this linear moment is exciting and most rewarding. We are coming to know of such contact and communication with your Earth realm and look forward to such opportunities. Know that your Spirit gains much insight and understanding from self with these connections as you call them. Be more within your inner self and let the true Spirit out to explore and grow in all ways. Let thy Spirituality flow from within naturally to gain more wisdom and knowledge than any other way. Meditate to gain access to many concepts, principles and truths beyond your imagination. Experience the Love and insights from within, for that is where you will find the truest form of truth and clarity. Many linear lifetimes of knowledge await you. When you allow such unfoldment to be as it should, that is when enlightenment happens.

Exist and be

Find this time in your linear experience to learn from such expressions of Love and Light imparting impressions upon you now. Be not concerned of past experiences, but be focused on this present moment. The present is all you truly have. Existing in the physical form is a true gift that must be lived with all emotions and opportunities of growth. Advancing your understanding of this life experience can only be done by living it and learn to your best ability, so you can feel the linear existence for all eternity. These impressions or memories as you call them, can and will be felt, seen, heard and all senses whenever you need them. Your natural sense of vibration will be activated the more you utilize it with ease. Be in the present to experience the truth of Love and what is possible from self. Be the Loving, Light that is within you, for there is no other way. When you do just that, your natural energetic field will be more colorful and bright. Allow what is truly possible to unfold naturally and the results for this linear existence will be astonishing.

Unknown signature

There is an energetic shift that comes to you now in this present moment. This time of your existence and Earth plane brings it to be now! The shift in Spiritual consciousness is at hand and comes at this time in which is most greatly needed. Be with this shift and allow yourself to experience this energetic vibration of heightened awareness. Be in the present to experience true Spirituality from within. Let the flow of natural energy create the energetic vibration and connection to the Divine Source and Original Energy. It is now to allow oneself to feel such Love and Light to bring forth growth on all levels of consciousness. Be the catalyst for change in these troubled times with Love and compassion for all. We are all Love and Light and that is what we are intended to permeate our essence of energy. Now is the time. Do not wait! The Positive energetic expression of now is activated and must be allowed to be revealed.

Let the unfoldment begin

We impart unto you our experiences, wisdom and knowledge to you in the physical. For there is much to be said and for you to learn in this linear lifetime. Opening up from within allows such growth and expansion of self. Be with Love and your Spirit to feel all there is to experience in this life and thy inner Soul. Feel the higher self grow from energetic vibrations of Love, Happiness, Forgiveness and true inner peace. Know thyself by allowing such experiences and expressions to unfold, for unexplainable growth in such a magnificent way that cannot be put into words. Experiences that cannot be proven or even explained are for your Spiritual growth and for you to share with anyone who will listen. Let the Spirit within take over, for such amazing experiences will happen even more regularly if you allow. The totality of these said expressions will be revealed to you in time.

Love, Exist

Feel the power of the energy within you and all around you at this very present moment. Be open to the energetic vibration that brings harmony and balance to your physical being. The true essence of self comes alive with Happiness and Love and awakens who you truly are. Be one with your inner self to experience all that is possible in the physical. The physical does have limitations, but you are more capable of these expressions and experiences if you do not have doubt. The possibilities are endless if you do not block such channels with the physical limitations. The energy is strong and thought provoking on a Spiritual level that it can be overwhelming in the physical. That is where you have to trust the Spirit within to know what is possible for you and not allow such limitations that you put on yourself to simply flow naturally. Be one with your eternal self and let the light brighten your path to grow in so many ways. Be Love and Light!! Do it now for your linear interferes with such expressions.

Unknown signature

Expressions of Love and Happiness come through with Positive energetic vibrations that flow from your being. This frequency that you vibrate at is allowing for such communications now. The true essence of self will allow one to truly experience all what is possible, if the physical allows. Be the one that encourages others and self to grow Spiritually with Love and Positivity in all aspects of this physical life. Do not close off the channels of growth and experiences by being closed minded in any regard. Do not judge others and situations that does not bring forth growth and positive change. Let the vibrations out and connect to everyone and everything, for it is here where the true Spirit will flourish. Know thy true self from within by allowing such expressions and experiences to unfold. For all wisdom and knowledge comes from these experiences, whether Positive or negative. Be in the present and live!!

Exist

Writing through and to you at this moment, brings such joy and opportunities for all involved with this experience. I will allow such knowledge to unfold for your growth on all levels. Be in the present with the physical to experience such expressions of Love, Growth and Harmonious times. Let the Spirit from within be in this very existence of linear and grow your Spirituality at an amazing rate. Yes we do vibrate at a faster and higher frequency, but we both vibrate energetically with Love. Let this Love lead you to a very fulfilled existence and allow such opportunities to expand your true inner self. Be whom you truly are and let the strong and powerful being out and grow to such levels of understanding beyond your wildest desires and imagination. Do it now and let the unfoldment succeed with Love and Growth. For there is where you find true enlightenment and calm.

Let your Spirit out

Your physical allows such opportunities to write and present material for Spiritual growth as well as human experiences for growing. Let the words flow and resonate with your Spirit, for it is meant to allow such expressions to assist you to flourish and learn from us. Take these words and make them to your understanding of how to improve your linear experiences of human existence. These times, as you call them, allow such opportunities to let these connections happen and be with them in the present. Put the focus on the present experience, for it will allow clarity and truth in time. Be with your Spirit from within to allow such unexplainable opportunities of growth on all levels and realms. Learning is an ongoing experience that is eternal and there are no quick, instant solutions that are event possible. These expressions and experiences unfold on their time and you are meant to experience these as a learning opportunity for growth on many levels. Allow the truth to unfold when the time is right to bring forth such growth and understanding. This happens in your paradigm when and if you are ready. Being open to allow these experiences to assist you on this journey of life is possible.

These human experiences are only complicated by the physical, not the Spiritual aspect from within. Let the true essence of self flourish, expand and grow in Love and prosperity on it's own accord. When you allow this naturally occurring events to unfold on their own, that is when you are in a very flowing, natural and harmonious flow with the Source! This is when you will feel truly connected with the Oneness.

All that is happening and will happen must be in order to clear out the negative, so the Positive can take over. The inner self awaits for opportunities to grow and be in such alignment with the Universe to be who one truly is and is meant to accomplish in this human experience and lifetime. Let the truth unfold and allow such possibilities to be you and your inner self, for that is where you will find the path, answers and understanding that you seek. Let life unfold as it should and the experience will be an amazing one. Love and live to the openness of what is possible. This time brings you understanding of this life and why you chose to have these experiences. When you have clarity and truth, then your shift will be in alignment with your outer and inner self as well as to Source. This brings about enlightenment and pure Spiritual awareness. When all is in alignment, life unfolds smoothly and naturally.

Be in Alignment

The time is now in the present to feel and act on the energetic vibrations of Love and Enlightenment. Allow these Positive energies to permeate such experiences for growth on all levels of consciousness. Be one with the Universe to feel the connection to everything. For we are all connected universally by the natural Laws of the Divine Source and Original Energy. These laws are simple and direct. They state we are all Love, Purity, Happiness and should allow such experiences to unfold for the better of everyone and everything. This energetic connectedness allows true self and understanding, not only for you, but for all who experience your vibrations. Live with purpose and passion and let the vibration of Love and Kindness lead this existence for Spiritual growth and life situations to unfold naturally. Be within yourself for such knowledge is waiting for you and for the truth to be told. Find the vibration that is you and let it unfold for Spiritual growth on all levels.

Unknown signature

This linear experience allows such accurate information to come through at this present moment. Be ready now to accept the Love and energetic connection to grow in more ways that could be expressed. Let the Spirit Within take the lead to allow such experiences and expressions of knowledge to expand the Universal Connectedness to learn what is truly possible. Feel the true essence of what is and let it lead the way for enlightenment and the gifts that have been bestowed upon you. Make others believe with Love and share what is learned in this lifetime to all who will listen. All that must be will come through now at a time of great turmoil and confusion on the Earth plane. Teach others the Spiritual way of Love and Positivity that will lead them to what is truly possible if one allows such expressions. The physical is more able than one allows it to be. Once you are on that frequency of Love and Positivity, your vibration will match a more natural state of flow.

Let Love through now

You are receiving this communication for our growth as well as yours. The Universal Energy Source provides all that you need to know for such beneficial experiences to enhance this lifetime. Come to accept and know these Loving Energies are Positive and for growth on all levels for not only in the physical, but Spiritually as well. This linear experience must feel all that will unfold to gather these reflections of time and space. Earth allows limited experiences because of the Physical, but not of the inner self for Spiritual growth. That essence of who we truly are is always accessible. Be one with everyone and everything, for we are all connected to the Divine Source. Let the abilities and gifts given to you do great work in helping others to grow in a Spiritual way and towards healing, if one allows. Healing comes from within and those wise enough to teach others the truth of what is. Go in Love, Kindness, Positivity to bring your true essence of pure bliss. Be happy and show others happiness.

Be in happiness

I find you and all who read these words are learning from this Positive Energy at this time. Learn from these communications from energies to bring forth growth on many levels. Be Loving to all including yourself to express the inner self knowledge that has been waiting for you to access it. Let the Spirit from within take you to higher advancements for enlightenment. In all regards to yearning for more, you must allow such vibrations to unfold as they will to bring Love and Light into all areas of this life experience. Let the Loving Energetic flow of life to take place to enhance all experiences in this lifetime. Growth and advancement is always available to you, if you allow such energies to unfold when it is time for the next level of transcendence. Be with your true self to know what is possible for Love and wonderful experiences to develop in the linear.

Be one with everything and everyone!

This linear experience leaves you with questions and concerns of *Biblical* events and future Earth events of great destruction??? The rapture and other predictions are all man-made religious events to give hope and fear to incarnate beings. To have such an experience would allow all man-made perceptions to be true, in which they are not! Do not allow such stories of impossible events to cloud your mind and emotions. These occurrences will not be and is Not possible to ever happen....... The great unknown is what you do not learn or seek to find answers to. This will be your down fall and create inner turmoil from within to seek such answers for what is not to be. The true answer is to live a Love based life, not a fear based life which religion advocates. When you live in the conscious awareness of Love and Positivity, the natural energetic flow of life just seems to be one with everyone and everything. Grow Spiritually and in the physical to allow such experiences to unfold as you feel such Love and Positive Energy to reveal itself in time. Do not let negative energy and your focus on these linear experiences waste your much valuable time on such events with grandiose proportions. These current events on Earth are at this current point and time, are what is the normal course to be at this linear expression. There will always be an Earth in some way and living creatures great and small will be.

To be continued on next page.

The worries and concerns of the now are wasted on events that will not happen. Live in the present to better oneself for growth and expansion on all levels. Let Love and Positivity lead the way, for that is where you will find the answers to what you seek. Be with your inner self to find peace and understanding of your existence at this present time. Love yourself, Love others, Forgive yourself, Forgive others. Forgiveness is one of the greatest energies to allow such expansion of understanding. Be kind and the current existence will be more wonderful than ever imagined. Go and live with Love and let the current matters of the world unfold as they should. Be quiet and still to allow the enjoyment this life has to offer before it is over. You will not see what you think is extreme in this lifetime. Be Loving, be kind, be forgiving and allow happiness now. And so it is...............

(These writings were channeled after a long afternoon talk with friends. One was quite religious and had lots of questions. I set the intention to do my session with questions concerning the Rapture and other religious concerns at that time. The last couple of pages were directed for the Rapture and other tragedies that are happening in this country and world right now.)

This is a time of Love and Clarity for you and all who read this. Confusion and strong energetic vibrations of concern and worry seem to control the masses at this linear experience. Allow Love and Positive energy to surround you and emanate these experiences to all whom you encounter. You feel uncertainty at this time and it feeds your inner fears. Remember the Love and Positivity bring about harmonious joy and expressions of understanding. Allow this unfoldment to be of great growth and expansion of energy to enlighten all who read this. Live with Love and Kindness, for such growth in all Spiritual levels will come through. Your Spirit within is who you truly are and allow that Spirit to fly free!! Have calm, clarity, truth and Love will bring about such abundance that you can't even fathom. Live with that Loving frequency to allow who and what you are!

Unknown signature

Now is the unfoldment of your next lessons of connecting to Spirit. You will have experiences for the first time and questions what this is and what it means. It is now for you to advance to the next level of transcendence of the energetic vibrations to experience the Totality of Love and assistance to others. You are a Spiritual being meant to help others and accept this as what you are to do from here on out in this linear lifetime! Being a Spiritual being affords you the enlightenment and clarity that most cannot see or understand, but you are to develop and exceed your possibilities to bring about hope and inner knowing for others. Be the physical one who does for others with Love and Positivity and bring forth all that is possible and let the Joy and Happiness be unleashed to them as it has been taken away in their lives. You have this ability now and it is time to spread the truth in your linear experiences to those in need. Go with Love and Truth and many will be helped in such a Loving and Positive way. And so it is......

(This particular session was telling me to take on this spiritual work as a full-time profession. I was still in denial about that possibility at the time but have since taken it on and it has been nothing but wonderful. When you listen to Spirit, amazing things happen.)

Let this energetic expression fill the space all around you in this linear point. Know that what is being received is for the highest and greatest good for all who experience these words. Your Paradigm is shifting into a Paradigm for the totality of what is possible when allowing oneself to receive. The beautiful silence from within is allowing the expansion of clarity and truth in the present time. Flowing with the linear expressions makes for a true inner frequency that is tuned into what is possible and probable for you. Allowing this frequency of Energy to flow like water that is going down stream is as natural as you living. Period! There is no secret that you in the physical seek, only Love and Positivity providing the clarity and truth that is. These linear expressions comes from a place with no time and no limits, if your being can allow such thoughts to be. Make your thoughts vibrate at a frequency of Love and Positive energy, then and only then can you truly be enlightened. The Spiritual path of awakening is at hand and is ready for your allowing now.

And so it is, Love

Receive these messages from Spirit and heed the clear and direct Loving messages that pertain to you. Allow the natural energetic flow to bring the words for you to understand our message to you at this linear expression. The paradigm is the conscious of clarity and truth which means for an enlightening experience, if one allows. Let the natural totality of frequency take you to a higher state of consciousness and understanding for all who read this. The most simplest of delivery of these transmissions is and will always be the best outcome of said messages. Live thy true self with Love, Positivity, Truth and Honesty, for there is no other way. For these vibrate at a very unique frequency bringing forth results in a very positive and productive way. Be in the state of allowing to receive truth and clarity about all matters concerning you in the physical. These experiences allow growth for all involved including you. Now is the linear experience of allowing to transcend to a higher understanding of what is possible. Let the true nature of energy flow freely through you and all around you. Love is from and for everyone and everything. Allow such Loving expressions to fill you and all in your environment.

Be the one to teach pure Love

These are just a few examples of automatic writing from me over the years. I have many journals filled with these writings, but I believe you get the clear picture. One of the most interesting things I've noticed is that the writings seem like they come from a different person or spirit. The words often appear to be very different from how I typically write and/or talk.

If this happens to you, it might initially surprise you, but do not be alarmed. It is perfectly normal to have what is written, for example, seem like someone else is writing. This is often a clear sign that you are communicating with Spirit during this time.

There have been times when I've had to look up an unfamiliar word's meaning. This often excites me as I know that Spirit is communicating from a higher dimension of consciousness. It's in sharp contrast to how we communicate in our everyday lives with very simple, direct language, using lots of slang and shortcuts.

If you have any questions on channeling or automatic writing, feel free to contact me through my website in the *About the Author* section. I often get lots of questions about what is written when people read the writings from Spirit.

Some of the writings are from those who were here on earth before. Some are from those who have never been anything other than in spirit form, which makes for interesting translation at times.

Chapter 6

Spirit is Energy

We are all energy. Everything and everyone is made up of Source energy and we all have a piece of it within us that connects to everything and everyone through Source. Once you realize this, you can begin to understand that Spirit is energy, and that particle of Source energy within us is called the soul.

That soul is an original piece of the Spirit that is you in totality. Your Spirit came from Source and your soul came from that Spirit, of which you are clearly a part. This soul that is in a human body - also known as the physical - is the energy that is eternal. Just by thinking about this very principle, it makes sense that we can communicate with Spirit after the physical body dies. The soul goes back to its original form in Spirit and takes with it the many memories and experiences from this lifetime and, of course, continues that loving energy. Remember, love never dies; neither does that connection.

So, we have determined that we are energy and that the energy that is you does not die; it simply transfers to its original spirit form, and in this form it is able to communicate.

The question, then, is: "How can it communicate?" The natural energetic state that is you is able to love and telepathically relay messages to their loved ones who are still in the physical. Often, the personality of the one who is now in spirit expresses itself in actions and behavior similar to how they were while alive in the physical. This is a way spirits validate it is them.

This expression can come in many forms, such as dreams, music, signs or billboards, license plates, electronic devices and, of course, wildlife. These are just some of the ways that they send messages to you that will make you unhesitatingly think of them.

The hardest part for us, who are still in a human body that is alive, is that we are often closed to this type of communication. Anyone has the natural ability to communicate with Spirit, if one so chooses. The key is to be open to the possibility and see what happens when you try to communicate with your loved ones who are now in Spirit.

At my seminars and workshops, I teach that you should start with basic meditation and set the intention to communicate with your loved one who is passed on. When you set a day and time to do just this, the energy of intention goes out to your loved one and they will prepare for such a connection.

Make sure you do this meditation session with them at this day and time to let them know you are serious. Make sure you are calm and ready for such an experience. Sometimes it can be very emotional and alarming that you feel them in this meeting.

It is also helpful to find the right setting for the meditation session. Perhaps you should think of a garden, a beach overlooking a lake, or a waterfall with comfy chairs facing the falls. Whatever would make you think of your loved ones and have you feel relaxed and safe is very important.

Remember you are in control of this connection. You can open your eyes and turn on the lights if you feel uncomfortable or upset. Please follow the protection example I outlined in Chapter One, or you can adapt it to suit your beliefs and needs. Remember, spirit communication should be done with love and positive energy for both you and who you want to communicate with. When the intention is done with this loving and positive energy, you will be safe, and good results can happen for you.

This energy is a part of all of us in the physical and in the spirit. The concept that we are all connected from the original Source energy should make this quite clear, or at least a bit clearer. Source can take on many forms by using its own energy and the energy of others.

I often feel drained after doing a gallery reading for a large audience, or after doing many private readings back to back. The energy comes from other places as well as from myself, so that is why I get physically tired. Energetically, both Spirit and I make this all possible with belief!

The energy I speak of is part of Source and everything, period! Once you grasp that concept of energy, that everything is made up of energy, and that everything is part of that Source energy, then this begins to make sense. Being open to these basic principles and concepts allows one to be able to access the doorway to spirit communication.

When you start the idea that you want to access this doorway to Spirit, make sure you have loving and positive intentions for such communications. When this is done with love and positivity, the results that you will get will be that very vibration of a loving energy to communicate with you. Your sincerity reveals the truth behind your intentions and you will attract that which is on your vibrational level or plain.

These communications should be from a loving, positive and knowledgeable expression. If this is not a helpful experience with love and positivity, then perhaps you should stop and reassess what you are doing specifically.

For example, if you did some automatic writing and the words that were written were negative and/or a fear-based message, then this is not helpful, in my opinion. What comes from Spirit should be loving and positive words to help you to grow as a person and as a spiritual being. You should feel good after you read what was written, not feel bad or even scared by what you experienced.

We are meant to grow in a positive way, as human beings and as spiritual beings. The life lessons that we learn help us and Source to evolve in a positive way for all involved. When you are happy and being positive about life, notice how good you feel. Everything seems to flow smoothly and simply fall into place.

On the other hand, when you are unhappy and are being negative, it seems to bring more of the same. For example, when you're having a bad day that seems to be getting worse, you could turn that around by saying "I am having a great day, starting right now!"

What you put out comes back, and when there is emotion and passion behind those feelings and words, it seems to come back instantly.

Even speaking the words out loud when you are upset or angry sends out strong vibrations of energy and it comes back quickly. Think about this the next time you have a bad day. Change your mood or bad day to a good day, just with your words and your emotional state. This does work, but you must be mindful of what you are saying and doing when you are in a bad place.

Simply acknowledging the energetic vibration you are putting out will help you in your everyday life. Your frequency is unique and when you become aware of this frequency that is your energy, you start to take control your life in a very positive way.

I ask you to try this experiment one day while shopping. Set the clear intention to be happy and feel fantastic as you go about your task and navigate through the store. You will see and feel how much nicer everyone is, and even more polite. Often you will smile more at others because you are being happy and positive; most will smile back at you. Ones that are usually rude and will not move their cart, often move for you as you go by. This experiment does work and will help bring awareness to you for your mood and the vibration you are putting out.

Now I ask you to do the same thing, but in the opposite way. Set the clear intention to feel negative and maybe even angry. Allow emotion to get behind this energy and go into the store. You will feel how very different everyone behaves, not only in and around the store, but towards you. You will be quite surprised by the behavior of others towards you and maybe even have them be rude. They often will not move their cart when you are going towards them and perhaps even frown at you as you go by. As soon as you get back to your car, set the clear intention to release these negative feelings and allow yourself to flow back to a positive, happy state of being.

This experiment does work. It will increase your awareness for the energy or frequency that you put out. And not just by your mood and the words coming out of your mouth, but also by what you are thinking.

This is another clear example of the Law of Attraction, expressed in common sayings such as "like attracts like" and "what you put out, you get back." You are a unique energy being and you can learn to control your mood with practice. Yes, you will have a bad day sometimes, and even a very bad experience, but how you react to each situation will help increase your awareness of these basic principles and concepts. You are capable of taking control of your life if you try to be mindful and want to be positive.

It is important to be aware of the energetic vibration that you put out in what you are saying, feeling and thinking. A negative can easily be turned to a positive, but the opposite is also true, so please be mindful each day of how and what you are attracting into your life by your thoughts.

Thoughts are things and they vibrate out at a certain frequency. Make sure those thoughts are positive and will help you. If you don't, what you are focusing on can be more harmful than you realize. By putting emotion into those thoughts, you can bring about a stronger vibration.

I want to end this chapter on a positive note. Know that you can put out the loving and positive energy each day, even when you sometimes make mistakes. We are human after all, so be mindful of those thoughts and what you're focusing on. This awareness will help you with your spirit communication as well.

The reason you need to understand the basic principles and concepts of energy is to benefit yourself and to ease your communication with Spirit. When you are feeling bad, or perhaps depressed, this is not the time to communicate with Spirit. You need to be in the most positive and loving place you can to experience communications with spirits.

You have passed loved ones in spirit, as well as spirit guides who will connect with you. When you connect with them, the more positive, loving and happy that you can be, the better the results and the more your vibration of positivity will attract them. The very vibration of love and positivity will bring about the highest and greatest good for you and your spirit communications.

Channeling and automatic writing must be done with that loving and positive energy to get the very best results, period! You only want those spirits and energies that are from a loving, positive place, and that vibrate at that frequency to be in your space. You would not invite negative people into your home who make you feel terrible and miserable, so don't allow such spirits to come into your space. This is a simple concept really, but one that is worth mentioning.

Chapter 7

Signs, Signals and Messages from Spirit

Any book about spirit communication needs to include discussion of the signs sent from Spirit or from our passed loved ones to us, still in the physical. When we lose a loved one and they physically die, we are often in a state of grieving. Be comforted knowing that our loved ones are still a part of our life and want to let us know that they are okay and doing just fine. We, who are left in the physical, may not be doing so well and sometimes can be in a very bad place. Hopefully, this book brings awareness that they who have passed are fine in Spirit, and that they can communicate with us.

We need to be open to receiving the messages and pay attention to the signs that are often presented to us. Be comforted knowing they contact us in many ways to get our attention and to have us think of them. When you grasp this concept, you will begin to notice the little subtleties and signs they send. Exciting, right? I think it is.

There are so many ways of communication to us here in the physical. If I went into such detail, I could write another book on the ways and how they do it. For now, let's simply state the obvious ways they communicate.

They love to come to us in our dreams. When you have a clear and vivid dream and know you were with them, you will remember the dream in great detail. The colors were more vivid and bright, the sensations were heightened. When you awake, you can often feel the sensations you felt in the dream: touch, smells, colors, emotions, etc.

This dream connection, as I call it, is usually filled with such happiness of being with them and experiencing spending time with them once again. The excitement and feelings from this dream are so intense that you know as a fact you were with them. This confirms it was a clear connection and not just an ordinary dream. When you relive the sense of touch or feel the emotion that you had during the dream, it brings such peace and happiness into your very being, that is absolutely time spent with your loved one who is now in Spirit.

These types of dreams can bring such peace and joy into your life when you know you had this experience. This is possible if you set the intention that you truly desire such. Do this with love, happiness and happy memories in your heart and you will make that intention even stronger. Spirits communicate best when there is love and happiness associated with the intention to connect with them, so be in a good place filled with happiness and joy towards them. Remember, love is the most positive and energetic vibration out there and can be felt by your loved ones. Think positive, loving thoughts when intending to connect.

You should keep a journal by your bed for such an occasion. Have a pen or pencil handy to write down what you experienced. As the day goes on, you might forget some important detail, so it is best to write it down as soon as you wake up.

Write down the date and time for keeping everything in proper order. The more often you have these dreams, the more you will see a pattern emerging with the message that is being sent to you. Be excited to know that they love us and still want to be a part of our lives, but they do not want to interfere with our free will of going on with our human life.

Dreams are an amazing way of connecting with our passed loved ones. Sometimes we are closed to that process by our grief or belief system, but if you allow the dream to come to you on its time and when you need it the most, it will happen. The dream will be most beneficial for you at the time that it is meant for you.

Another way that spirits communicate with us is with smells. They often send to us a strong scent of perfume or cologne, or even cigarette or cigar smells. Flowers such as roses or carnations can be used to get our attention. When these smells come into our space, they make us think of our passed loved ones and we can often then feel their presence. Just knowing that they are with us might bring a cold chill or perhaps a misty or cloudy look in the air.

This is them reassuring us that they are okay and still around watching over us. These smells will make us think of them without hesitation and are their way of getting our attention. Our loved ones can be very clever with these smells when they wish to get our attention, often using the most common smell that would be uniquely associated with them.

They can even have the smell just be in the room that you are in. If you go to investigate other rooms or areas of the house, you may find that the smell is only in the room that you smelled it in. It may linger for an hour or a minute, depending on your receptivity to the experience. My favorite smells are those that recall a loving memory. Whenever this happens for you, say thank you, and send them your love. They can feel it from you.

Number sequences can be a sign from loved ones, too. They can send us numbers like 222, or a specific time, such as 11:11, as a way to get our clear attention and think of them. The same number and time might recur once or twice a day, or the number sequence may happen daily and more often. When the numbers and other events seem to fall into alignment with one another, it is called synchronicity.

The numbers could have no exact meaning, other than to get our attention, or they could, for instance, indicate the time of their passing. I have had the numbers 11:11 shown to me every day for years since my mom passed. She used to wake me up every morning between 3:00am and 3:30 am, and I always felt like she was there or had been there just before I woke up. This did not match the time of her passing, but I always felt the strong connection to my mom.

The number sequences could also be from your spirit guides letting you know that you're on the right track. For example, if you see 111, 222, 333, 444 and 555 every day, they are telling you something. The numbers are in our everyday life and get our attention when they appear to us in a repetitive manner. Spirit is quite clever with using numbers to get our undivided attention.

A very fun way Spirit communicates with us is through electronic devices. Since we are all energy and Spirit is pure energy, it only makes sense that they can manipulate energetic devices such as radios, TVs, computers and other electrical components. They seem to love to flick lights or dim a light bulb to get our attention. When this happens, if you think of your passed loved one right away, it is definitely their attempt to get your attention.

We have an Alexa in several rooms of our home which seems to go off for no reason, often saying words and phrases that she normally does not use. When she pops on and says the time or answers a question out of the blue, I know it is from Spirit and almost always from family in spirit.

Family seems to enjoy turning off the TV for no particular reason when we are talking about them, as if to say, "We are here." The light bulb above the stove sends clear signals from my husband's dad in spirit.

I always find it interesting when my cell phone acts funny for no reason, or it fails to record something or take a picture. At other times I feel compelled to hit record and get amazing footage when I view it later. The ability to manipulate electronic devices seems very easy for them and almost natural. When you experience this, say hello and send them your love. They know you will feel it is from them, and acknowledging it makes them quite happy.

There is always something special about music and songs that remind us of our loved ones in spirit. A song can make us think of them within a second and we know it is from them to us.

There seems to be such emotion behind a song that brings back happy memories, or a song that was played at the funeral. Crying and laughing are just a few of the emotions that a simple song can evoke.

Have you ever thought about your passed loved one and then their song came on? I'm sure you have, and you know instantly it was sent from them. They can and do play music meant for us when we are thinking of them, whether we are missing them in a sad mood or having a fond memory and quite happy. That song can transport us from sad to happy in a blink of an eye but can do the opposite as well. Hopefully, you can think of them with the songs that remind you of them in a happy and loving way, for that is how they want you to think of them.

The same can be said of TV shows, movies or programs that they loved to watch. You could be scrolling through the stations when something stops you from channel surfing and you go right to the program that they always watched. Allow yourself to watch and think of them with love and happy memories.

Healing can come as you remember them with the TV movies and programs that they watched. Allow a little time to see these programs as gentle reminders that they still are watching over you and seeing what you are looking at on the TV.

Wildlife is another communication form that many of us have experienced. The most common is with birds, such as the red cardinal. Many have heard that if you see a red cardinal, it is a sign from your recent passed loved one. The birds can be any type that would make you think of your passed loved one, whether it is a cardinal, blue jay, robin and, of course, hummingbirds. Next to the famous red cardinal is the hummingbird. This bird signifies the light and free motion of your loved one in spirit. This bird can fly backwards and teaches us we can look back on our past but must not dwell on it. We need to move forward.

Eagles represent guardians. They can bear messages to and from the Divine Source, inspire wisdom, manifest well-being and offer us insight. Just watching an eagle soar above can be a message from the universe to pay closer attention to your inner voice and to trust it.

Hawks represent a message from angels and they are telling you to open your awareness wide. When a hawk swoops into your life, be ready for a whole new awareness in spirit. Hawks are associated with your soul and let you know to have great vision in the present moment.

Butterflies are a great reminder that we can transition into something better and are flying free. When you see a butterfly, it is time for mental and spiritual growth. You cannot embrace the new you, until you release the old.

Dragonflies call to your flexibility and a fresh perspective is needed. Dragonflies are thought to be messengers from the spiritual world. The little flying creatures teach us to live each moment to the fullest. Be aware of all the gifts and lessons you encounter daily.

Deer are another great example that signifies you are being contacted from passed loved ones in spirit. I had my very own encounters every day for a month after my mom passed. The deer would come to the end of our fence and look straight into our sliding glass door every morning between 9am – 9:15am. I would go outside onto the back deck and talk to the deer as if mom was there. I knew mom sent the deer to me every day, so I could communicate with her.

The deer would just stare at me and seemed to pay attention to what I was saying. When I started to cry, the deer would turn its head and stare at me even more intently. Mom use to feed the deer every day for more than twenty years in her old home. I remember looking out on some afternoons and would see dozens of them eating. Mom knew I would think of her when this deer came by every morning.

One morning, for example, as we were waking up I noticed from our bedroom window a doe and her fawn were walking right next to each other. They walked within a few feet of my bedroom window. When they saw me, they just looked at me for a minute and slowly walked off. Wildlife can be manipulated by Spirit to send us a message, saying "I am fine, remember me, I love you."

Another example of spirit communication is finding coins that would make you think of your loved ones. The ability to make these coins appear in your path is quite amazing and possible. How they do it, I do not know, but they can. You might find the coins from the year they were born or the year that they passed. I believe they will send the type of coin to make you think of them and it will be from a year that you would associate with them.

When you find a feather, this is a magical way of Spirit communicating with you, showing support and guidance. It is also another cosmic hello. Feathers fall into your path from the Divine Source and are sent your way to comfort you and place you in a state of joy and higher awareness.

If you find a white feather, that can represent that your loved one in spirit is watching over you and at peace. It is their way to send you a message from the other side.

All these ways of spirit communication make you think of your loved one. They will send you exactly what you need so you'll know it is from them. This can be any of these many examples and more besides. Know that your passed loved ones will go out of their way to comfort you with these beautiful signs, signals and messages from the spirit world. Just please be open to seeing them and know they are from them. Thank them and send them your love.

Here is another example of spirit communication. Often you hear about someone who lost their mom, for example, and she called out their name. This would startle most people, if not outright scare them, but this even happened to me the first night after my mom's passing. I heard my name said out loud as I was lying in bed. I searched the whole house looking for my mom and did not see her.

This is something that does happen, and I hope it does not scare the person that it happens to. They are just letting you know that they are okay and still watching over you.

Hearing your name called by someone who passed recently can be upsetting and even frightening, but know it is not meant to be. Tell them you love them, and you heard them calling you.

Some people report seeing their passed loved ones standing at their bed or in another room soon after they transitioned into Spirit. Typically, you see them with your peripheral vision. When you do, they are just checking in on you to see that you are okay. When you try to look directly, however, the vision usually goes away.

This is quite an occurrence for some, while to others it is no big deal. Whichever way you interpret this, be comforted that your passed loved ones are letting you know that all is well and they are still a part of your life.

Our loved ones do communicate with us through signs, signals and messages. They use wildlife, music, light bulbs flickering, electronic devices, smells and more. Pay attention and you will experience the signs as well.

Love never dies; neither does that connection.

Chapter 8

Energy and the Law of Attraction

As we discussed in Chapter Six, everything is made up of energy and vibrates at a certain rate. There is constant motion in everything and everyone. These basic principles and concepts should make you more aware now that spirit communication is possible since it is in pure spiritual energy and we are also part of that energy, which we call the soul.

The frequency that is put out from Spirit vibrates at a much faster rate than we who are still in physical form. The ability to communicate with Spirit can be summed up by this basic principle: Human beings must raise their vibrations to communicate with Spirit; Spirit must lower theirs to communicate. Hence the name "medium," which comes from the Latin word for "middle." We meet in the middle for spirit communication. In a sense, you are doing mediumship when you communicate with Spirit. Pretty cool, right?

Thought is energy. The source of all power and all life is with thought. Thought is a spirit activity. This book has demonstrated several ways that the Divine Spirit or Original Energy can work through us to communicate.

The Divine Spirit is always around us and within us. In fact, it is us. We are all made of energy that originated from the Divine Source. This is a very powerful realization.

The Divine Source formed a universe that operates on a very exact set of universal laws. These universal laws are neutral and affect every person in the exact same way; no one is exempt. Once these laws are recognized and learned they can be used to our advantage.

The laws are always working, whether we are aware of them or not. It is like the Law of Gravity: It does not apply only to those who know about it, but it applies to everyone equally. These laws have created the universe that we live in. They have not only been around since the start of time, they were what started time.

The law that I would like to focus on is the Law of Attraction and how it relates to communicating with the spirit world. Most people who have an interest in communicating with Spirit have at least heard of the Law of Attraction and are somewhat familiar with how it works.

Basically, the Law of Attraction means that like attracts like and that what we think about we bring about. Our thoughts are pure energy and we can change our lives just by changing our thoughts. We also use our thoughts to allow the Divine Spirit and our spirit guides to work though us.

The Law of Attraction is a direct connection to Spirit. As our thoughts go out into the universe they are received by the Divine Spirit and our spirit guides. In return, the Divine Spirit and our spirit guides will bring the opportunities that we need to accomplish our dreams, goals and desires. The Divine Spirit uses our human vessel to manifest everything that is existence.

This is why it is so important to focus on what you want to manifest. The Divine Spirit is neutral and reacts to all our thoughts, whether positive or negative. The more we are open to the process and remain positive, the more the Divine Spirit can use our human vessel and work though us. In return, we are rewarded in many ways. It could be financial, emotional or spiritual.

There are many ways to activate the Law of Attraction to allow the Divine Source to work though us. One of the most effective ways is through future visualization. When we visualize our future exactly the way we would like it to be we are sending out thought energy to the Divine Source and to our spirit guides.

Our spirit guides and the Divine Source will then present us with the opportunities we need to manifest that future into reality. Everything that has ever been manifested was first a thought or idea that was then acted upon.

Think of visualization as a mind movie of your perfect future. Many of the greatest thinkers of all time have used this technique. Visualization does take a little bit of practice and may seem awkward at first, but it is actually quite fun.

Find a quiet space where you will not be distracted. Concentrate on your breathing, becoming aware of each breath that you take. Close your eyes and mentally see your future as you would like it to be, whether it's the type of house you live in, the car you drive, or your career and the amount of money you make.

This is your imagination at play. Make it fun and exciting. Dream big! Let the Divine Source know that you are ready to receive all that is in your mind movie and that you are ready for the opportunities to make it a reality.

As you repeatedly watch your mind movie, you will start to see your spirit guides and the Divine Source at work, showing you scenes of what is possible for you and what your life could be. Your purpose will also be revealed to you.

As the details become clearer, so will your passions and purpose. It is very important to pay attention to the details in your mind movie. This is Divine Source communicating directly to you.

You must believe that if it is in your mind movie, it is possible for you. The Divine Source will not give you a dream or goal without a path to achieve it. Watch your future mind movie at least twice daily and always before going to sleep at night. Then, be ready for the opportunities that will come your way.

Keep a notepad by your bedside and be ready to jot down ideas that come to you in your sleep. The Divine Source often communicates to us through our dreams.

When working with the Divine Source to activate the Law of Attraction, always be ready to take action. Ideas without action are wasted. The Divine Source will present opportunities, but you will have to do the work and put in the effort.

When a negative thought pops into your head, as it will from time to time, counteract it with a positive thought. Always expect the best outcome. There will still be some negative outcomes because we cannot control the thoughts and free will of others, but by always keeping your thoughts positive you will create positive results.

Another way to activate the Law of Attraction is with positive affirmations, the most powerful being: "I am"

> I am abundant
>
> I am successful
>
> I am able to create my future
>
> I am living the life of my dreams
>
> I am in a wonderful relationship
>
> I am healthy
>
> I am able to overcome obstacles
>
> I am joyful
>
> I am thankful
>
> I am love
>
> I am part of the Original Source
>
> I am energy

When using "I am" affirmations always speak out loud with enthusiasm and in the present tense. You are acknowledging your readiness for the Divine source to work though you.

I make up my own affirmations to start my day. For example:

Today is the greatest day of my life!

I feel fantastic, I feel wonderful, I feel amazing!

Something amazing is going to happen to me today!

I feel so healthy and full of energy!

After I state these affirmations out loud, I then raise my hands in the air with excitement. This brings more positive, happy energy into these affirmative statements. Have fun with it and make it a great daily habit for yourself.

We are all part of the Divine Source or original energy. We already have within in us everything we need to live the life of our dreams. Our thoughts are the link between our human vessel and the original energy. All thoughts are energy. They are the conduit between us and the spirit world.

We originated from the original Source and when our time in this human vessel is over we will return to original Source. Energy never dies. Once we fully comprehend this, we see how our thoughts connect us to Spirit.

We can use the Law of Attraction to allow the Divine Source to work though us. Using our thoughts, we can communicate with our spirit guides and the Divine Source to create the exact life we want to live and discover our true purpose. The Divine Source is not only working through us; It is us. We are all one.

I wish you well

Conclusion

In conclusion, I would like to remind everyone that this book has some thought-provoking ideas, principles and concepts about communicating with Spirit. When done with love and positivity, the results are always better.

Try some of the ways that I mentioned in this book and have fun with them. For some, it will come easily; others will need extra time. Allow yourself to be patient with the results, as they vary with each person.

Remember, we are all individuals with that unique essence making us, us. That unique energy that is connected to everything and everyone reacts differently to these different ways of communicating to Spirit.

Allow the experiences to unfold naturally and you will get the very best results. I wish you well in this fun experience of communicating with Spirit.

Remember, love never dies; neither does that connection.

About the Author

Ashley Marsillas is an intuitive psychic medium and spiritual teacher. She has done readings for hundreds of clients over the years, as well as leading large spiritual events. Ashley writes daily and has several books planned for publication.

She regularly gives private readings and continues to present workshops and seminars teaching spirituality and meditation around the Midwest.

You may contact Ashley or get more information about the subjects in this book by visiting her website at:

www.thewisconsindellsmedium.com